I0004567

UNIX
Commands

Including

50 plus most commonly used UNIX Commands
Useful for both
Beginners and Experienced Professionals

(Author- Niraj Gupta)

Table of Contents

Introduction to UNIX

1) The UNIX operating system is a set of programs that act as a link between the computer and the user.
2) UNIX is a computer Operating System which is capable of handling activities from multiple users at the same time. Hence UNIX is called a multiuser system.
3) A user can also run multiple programs at the same time; hence UNIX is called multitasking.
4) UNIX has been found to be a very robust and reliable operating system. Unlike some of the other operating systems, UNIX rarely, if ever, crashes with memory or segmentation problems.
5) It is a highly portable operating system. Having been written in C, as against assembly language, it is independent of any particular hardware architecture. This also leads to software portability, i.e., a software developed using a Unix system can be easily ported to any other Unix system, even if the other system is on a different hardware architecture.

UNIX Operating System

Kernel

1) The kernel of UNIX is the hub of the operating system: it allocates time and memory to programs and handles the file store and communications in response to system calls.
2) The computer program that allocates the system resources and coordinates all the details of the computer's internal is called the operating system or kernel.
3) Kernel interacts with hardware and most of the tasks like memory management, task scheduling and file management.
4) Allocate time and memory to programs,
5) Handles storage of files etc.

Shell

1) When a user logs in, the login program checks the username and password, and then starts another program called the shell.
2) Users communicate with the kernel through a program known as the shell.
3) The shell is the utility that processes your requests.
4) The shell is a command line interpreter; it translates commands entered by the user and converts them into a language that is understood by the kernel.
5) The shell uses standard syntax for all commands,
6) C Shell, Bourne Shell and Korn Shell are most famous shells which are available with most of the UNIX variants.

The tcsh shell has certain features to help the user inputting commands.

Filename Completion - By typing part of the name of a command, filename or directory and pressing the [Tab] key, the tcsh shell will complete the rest of the name automatically. If the shell finds more than one name beginning with those letters you have typed, it will beep, prompting you to type a few more letters before pressing the tab key again.

History - The shell keeps a list of the commands you have typed in. If you need to repeat a command, use the cursor keys to scroll up and down the list or type history for a list of previous commands.

As an illustration of the way that the shell and the kernel work together, suppose a user types **rm myfile** (which has the effect of removing the file **myfile**). The shell searches the file store for the file containing the program **rm**, and then requests the kernel, through system calls, to execute the program **rm** on myfile. When the process **rm myfile** has finished running, the shell then returns the UNIX prompt % to the user, indicating that it is waiting for further commands.

Commands and Utilities

1) There are various command and utilities which you would use in your day to day activities.
2) cp, mv, cat and grep etc. are few examples of commands and utilities.

Files and Directories

1) Everything in UNIX is either a file or a process.
2) All data in UNIX is organized into files.
3) All files are organized into directories.
4) These directories are organized into a tree-like structure called the file system.
5) All the files are grouped together in the directory structure. The file-system is arranged in a hierarchical structure, like an inverted tree. The top of the hierarchy is traditionally called **root** (written as a slash /)

Signing on to UNIX

The UNIX system administrator creates account for various users of the system with a user name and password. The user can enter into the UNIX system using those login credentials. After successfully logging in to the UNIX system, the system displays the dollar sign ("**$**") as the prompt, with the cursor (_) constantly blinking beside it. This is UNIX's prompt, and UNIX systems mostly feature the **$** as the default prompt.

UNIX Commands

1. CAT: Concatenate files to standard output

   The "cat" command can be used to:

   - Display text files
   - Copy text files into a new document
   - Append the contents of a text file to the end of another text file, combining them

   Syntax:

   cat [options] [file_names]

   Example:

   $ cat myfile.txt

   This command will display the contents of the text file "myfile" on the screen.

   $ cat myfile.txt > mynewfile.txt

   This command will read the contents of myfile.txt and send them to standard output; instead of displaying the text, however, the shell will redirect the output to the file mynewfile.txt. If mynewfile.txt does not exist, it will be created. If mynewfile.txt already exists, it will be overwritten and its previous contents will be lost, so be careful.

   $ cat myfile.txt >> mynewfile.txt

   This command will read the contents of myfile.txt, and write them at the end of mynewfile.txt. If mynewfile.txt does not already exist, it will be created and the contents of myfile.txt will be written to the new file.

   $ cat myfile1.txt myfile2.txt > mynewcombinedfile.txt

   This command will concatenate 2 text files myfile1.txt and myfile2.txt and write them to a new file mynewcombinedfile.txt.

   $ cat –n myfile1.txt myfile2.txt > mynewcombinedfile.txt

   -n will number all output lines from file mynewcombinedfile.txt.

2. CD: Change directory

   The "cd" command allows you to change your working directory. You use it to move around within the hierarchy of your file system.

   Example:

   $ cd

   Or

$ cd ~

These commands will put you in your home directory.

$ cd.

This command will leave you in the same directory you are currently in (i.e. your current directory won't change).

$ cd ~username

This command will put you in username's home directory.

$ cddir (without a /)

This command will put you in a subdirectory. for example, if you are in /usr, typing cd bin will put you in /usr/bin, while cd /bin puts you in /bin.

$ cd ..

This command will move you up one directory. So, if you are /usr/bin/tmp, cd ..moves you to /usr/bin, while cd ../.. moves you to /usr (i.e. up two levels). You can use this indirection to access subdirectories too. So, from /usr/bin/tmp, you can use cd ../../local to go to /usr/local.

$ cd −

This command will switch you to the previous directory (UNIX only). For example, if you are in /usr/bin/tmp, and go to /etc., you can type cd - to go back to /usr/bin/tmp. You can use this to toggle back and forth between two directories.

3. CHMOD: Change access permissions

The "chmod" command is used to change the permissions of files or directories.

Example:

$ chmod u=rwx,g=rx,o=r file1

This command allows the owner to set the following permissions

- The user can read, write, and execute the file
- Members belonging to your group can read and execute the file
- Others may only read the file.

  o   u - user, g - group, o - other
  o   r - read, w - write , x - execute

$chmod 754 file1

This command is equivalent to the command used above. The permissions for the user, group and others are represented by the digits 7, 5 and 4. Each digit is a combination of numbers 4, 2, 1 and 0

4 - "read", 2 - "write", 1 - "execute", 0 - "no permission"

4. CHOWN: Change file owner and group

The "chown"command is used to change the owner and owning group of a file.

Examples:

$ chown root /var/run/httpd.pid

Change the owner of /var/run/httpd.pid to 'root' (the standard name for the Superuser).

$ chownrob:developers strace.log

Change the owner of strace.log to 'rob' and the group identifier to 'developers'.

$ chown -R foouser base

Change the ownership of base to the user foouser and make it recursive (-R)

$ chown -R newuser:newgroup .

Change the ownership to newuser and group to newgroup for all of the files and directories in current directory, and all subdirectories (recursively).

5. CHGRP: Changing group

The "chgrp" command is used for changing groupownership of a file or files.

Examples:

$ chgrp hope file.txt

Change the owning group of the file file.txt to the group named hope.

$ chgrp -hR staff /office/files

Change the owning group of /office/files, and all subdirectories, to the group staff.

6. CKSUM: Print CRC checksum and byte counts

The "cksum" command is used to checksum and counts the bytes in a file.

Example:

$ cksum myfile.txt

This command calculates the checksum and byte count of myfile.txt and output the values along with the filename.

Output:

3042891102 56 myfile.txt

Where "3042891102" represents the checksum value and "56" represents the file size of myfile.txt.

7. CMP: Compare two files

The "cmp" command is used to compare two files of any type and writes the results to the standard output. By default, cmp is silent if the files are the same; if they differ, the byte and line number at which the first difference occurred is reported.

Example:

$cmp myfile1.txt myfile2.txt

This command will compare myfile1 to myfile2, reading each file byte-by-byte and comparing them until one of the byte pairs is not equal. When a difference is found, it will output the location in the file where the difference was found, and exit.

Output:

Myfile1.txt myfile2.txt differ: char 1001, line 99

8. CP: Copy one or more files to another location

This "cp" command is used for copying files and directories.

Example:

$ cp myfile1.txt myfile2.txt

Through this command myfile1.txt will be copied to myfile2.txt, where myfile1.txt is the source of copy operation and myfile2.txt is the destination.

The source and destination files may also reside in different directories.

For example:

$ cp /home/test/data/ myfile1.txt /home/test/backup/myfile1.txt

9. DU: Estimate file space usage

The "du" command is used to estimate file space usage—space used under a particular directory or files on a file system.

Examples:

$ du -sk *

Where, (-s) is the Sum of directories (-k) is kilobytes

Output:

123546 directoryOne
1896545 directoryTwo

$ du -sh *

Where, (-s) is the Sum of directories in human-readable format and (-h) can be Byte, Kilobyte, Megabyte, Gigabyte, Terabyte or Petabyte.

Output:
123M directoryOne
1.2G directoryTwo

$du -shc *.txt

This command will report the size of each file in a human-readable format, and also displays a grand total.

6.0K   myfile1.txt
2.0K   myfile2.txt
10.0K   myfile3.txt
18.0K   total

10. DF: Display free disk space

The "df" Command is used to report the amount of available disk space being used by file systems.

Examples:

$ df

This command will display all the file systems and their disk usage.

$ df –h

This command is same as above, but use "human readable" formatting.

$ dfmytest_dir

This command will display the amount of free space in the mytest_dir directory.

11. FILE: Determine type of file

The "file" command is used for recognizing the type of data contained in a computer file.

Examples:

$ file *.txt

This command will list any files ending with extension .txt

12. FUSER: Identify process using file

The "fuser" command is used to show which processes are using a specified file, file system, or UNIX socket. fuser displays the PIDs of processes using the specified files or file systems.

Example:

$ fuser .

This command will display every process ID that is using the current directory ("./").

13. LS: List information about file(s)

The "ls" command is used to list the files and directories stored in the current directory.

Syntax: $ ls

Ls −l command: lists your files in 'long format', which contains lots of useful information, e.g. the exact size of the file, who owns the file and who has the right to look at it, and when it was last modified.

Syntax : $ ls −l

Ls −a command: List the current directory including hidden files. Hidden files start

with "."

Syntax: $ ls -a

Ls −x command: This command displays the list of files/folders in horizontal format.

Syntax: $ ls -x

Ls –lt command: This command lists the files/folders with the recently accessed file/folder at the top.

Syntax: $ ls -lt

Ls * command: "*" is a meta character. We use * to match 0 or more characters.

Syntax: $ ls *.doc

(Displays all the files that ends with .doc)

Ls ?command: "?" is also a meta character. A question mark (**?)** Matches with single character.

Syntax: $ ls ???

Displays all the files in the current directory whose names are only three characters long.

14. MKDIR: Create new folder(s)

The "mkdir" command is used to make a new directory.

Example:

$ mkdirmydir_name

This command will create a new directory i.e. "mydir_name".
$ mkdir-p/tmp/a/b/c

This command will create multiple directories.

I.e. If /tmp/a exists but /tmp/a/b does not, mkdir will create /tmp/a/b before creating /tmp/a/b/c.

15. MV: Move or rename files or directories

The "mv" command is used to move one or more files or directories from one place to another. If both filenames are on the same file system, this results in a simple file rename; otherwise the file content is copied to the new location and the old file is removed.

Example:

$ mvmyfilemynewfilename

This command rename "myfile" to "mynewfilename".

$ mvmyfile ~/myfile

This command will move "myfile" from the current directory to the user's home directory.

16. PWD: Print working directory

The "pwd" command is used to output the path of the current working directory.

Examples:

$ pwd

Output: /home/mydir

This command prints out the "/home/mydir", that means that the directory the user is currently in is /home/mydir.

17. RM: Remove (delete) files

The "rm" command is used to remove/delete files or directories.

Example:

$ rm myfile.txt

This command will delete the file "myfile.txt".

$ rm -i myfile.txt

This command will prompt for confirmation before actually removing it.

18. RMDIR: Remove folder(s)

The "rmdir" command is used to remove the empty directory.

Example:

$ rmdirmydir

This command will remove the "mydir" directory

19. KILL: Stop a process from running

The "kill" command can be used to send signals to running processes in order to request the termination of the process

Example:

$ kill 111

This command terminates the process with process id '111'.

$ kill all

This command kills all the process and the server goes for a restart.

20. TIME: Measure Program Resource Use

The "time" command is used to determine the duration of execution of a particular command.

Example:

$ timels

This command will report how long it took to execute the ls command in terms of user CPU time, system CPU time, and real time.

21. CLEAR: Clear terminal screen

The "clear" command is used to clear the screen.

Example:

$ clear

22. EXIT: Exit the Shell

Issuing the "exit" command at the shell prompt will terminate running jobs and cause the shell to exit.

Example: $exit

Common aliases for exit are: "bye", "logout", and "lo".

23. LOGNAME: Print current login name

The "logname" command is used to print the name of the user executing the command.

Example;

$ logname

This command returns the name of the currently logged in user.

24. PASSWD: Modify a user password

The "passwd" command is used to change a user's password.

Example:

$ passwd username

This command is used to Change the password for the user named "username".

25. SU: Substitute user identity

The "su" command can be used to switch user to that of super user or another user.

Example:

$ su user2

This command can be used to login as user2 by entering the password. 'exit' can be used to exit from it.

26. TALK: Chat to Users

The "talk" command is used to chat with another logged-in user(s) or allow chat to users on other systems.

Example:

$ talk user3

This command will allow the current user to talk to user "user3".

27. UNAME: Print system information

The "uname" command is used to print the name, version and other details about the current machine and the operating system running on it.

Example:

$ uname –a

This command displays system information.

28. W: Who is logged on

The "w" command is a quick way to see who is logged on and what they are doing.

Example:

$ w

This command will show a list of logged on users and their processes.

$ w user1

This command will show information for the user named "user1".

29. WALL: Write to all

The "wall" command is used to write messages to other logged-in users. This command can be used by root to send out shutting down message to all users just before power off.

Example;

$ wall

Write you message here.

^D

30. WHO/WHO AM I: Print all usernames currently logged in / Print the current user id and name

The "who" command displays a list of all users who are currently logged into the computer.

Example:

$ who

This command displays the username, line, and time of all currently logged-in sessions.

Output:

```
Sam     pts/1      2014-01-17 22:42 (:0.0)
Ruby    pts/2      2014-01-18 09:30 (:0.0)
Karan   pts/3      2013-12-25 08:52 (:0.0)
John    pts/4      2014-01-05 15:33 (:0.0)
Paul    pts/0      2013-09-04 22:05 (:0.0)
```

$ who am i

This command displays the same information, but only for the terminal session where the command was issued.

Output:

Sam   pts/1   2014-01-17 22:42 (:0.0)

31. WRITE: Write Messages to other Users

The "write" command is used to write messages to another user.

Example:

$ write user1 pts/1

Test Message.

This command is used to write a message to the user "user1" on terminal pts/1.

Will show up to the user on that console as:

Message from root@punch on pts/1 at 11:19 ...
Test Message

32. BASENAME: Delete prefix up to last slash

The "basename" command is used to delete any prefix up to the last slash ('/') character and return the result.

Example:

$ basename /home/paul/base.txt

Output: base.txt

This command will retrieve the last name from a pathname ignoring any trailing slashes.

$ basename /

Output:
/

33. COMM: Compare two sorted files line by line

The "comm" command is used to compare two files for common and distinct lines. I.e. Compare two sorted files line-by-line.

Example:

File 1: Fruit1.txt

apple
banana
eggplant

File 2: Fruit2.txt

apple
banana
zucchini

$ comm -12 fruit1.tx fruit2.txt

Output:

apple
banana

This command prints only the lines present in both fruit1.txt and fruit2.txt.

34. DIFF: Display the differences between two files

The "diff" command can be used to compare two files, and it will show the contents where they differ.

Example:

$ diff file1 file2

This command compares file1 and file2 and displays the difference.

35. DIRNAME: Convert a full pathname to just a path

When "dirname" is given a pathname, it will delete any suffix beginning with the last slash ('/') character and return the result

Example:

$ dirname /home/mydir/docs/

Output:

/home/mydir

This command will retrieve the directory-path name from a pathname ignoring any trailing slashes.

36. ED: A line-oriented text editor

The "ed" command is the standard UNIX text editor. It is used to create, display, modify and otherwise manipulate text files.

Example:

$ ed filename.txt

This command will open a file "filename.txt" for any editing.

37. JOIN: Join lines on a common field

The "join" command is used to join the lines of two files which share a common field of data.

Example:

File1.txt

John Raj
Sam Paul

File2.txt

John Sameer
Pal   Karan

$ join file1.txt file2.txt

Output:

John Raj Sameer

This command will display the above data as "John" is a common as a first word of both files.

38. NL: Number lines and write files

The "nl" command is used for numbering the lines from a file.

Example:

File1.txt

Abc
Def
Ghi
Jkl
Mno

$ nl file1.txt

Output:

```
1 Abc
2 Def
3 Ghi
4 Jkl
5 Mno
```

This command is used to number each line and display the result to standard output.

39. PASTE: Merge lines of files

The "paste" command is used to display the corresponding lines of multiple files side-by-side.

Example:

File1.txt

John Raj
Sam Paul

File2.txt

8898
2345

$ paste file1.txt file2.txt

Output:

John Raj 8898
Sam Paul 2345

This command displays the corresponding lines of file1.txt and file2.txt side-by-side.

40. SORT: Sort text files

The "sort" command is used to sort the contents of the file numerically or alphabetically.

Example:

File1.txt

apples
oranges
pears
kiwis
bananas

$ sort file1.txt

Output:

apples
bananas
kiwis
oranges
pears

This command will sort the lines in file "file1.txt" alphabetically.

41. SPELL: Check misspelled words

The "spell" command is used for spell-checking program which scans a text file for misspelled words, and prints each misspelled word on its own line.

Example;

File1.txt

Thisz is a test message
Find out all the miztakes

File2.txt

This iz a test message
Find outz all the mistakes

$ spell –on file1.text file2.txt

[-o is used to print the filename and –n is used to print line number of each misspelled word]

Output:

File1.txt:1: thisz
File1.txt:2: miztakes
File2.txt:1:iz
File2.txt:2: outz

This command displayed the file and line number along with the misspelled words.

42. TR: Translate, squeeze, and/or delete characters

The "tr" command is used to translate/substitute sets of characters.

Example:

$ tr "[:lower:]" "[:upper:]" < file1.txt

This command will translate the contents of "file1.txt" to uppercase.

43. UNIQ: Uniquify files (remove all duplicate lines)

The "uniq" command is used to filter out repeated lines in a file.

File1.txt

This is line1
This is line1

This is line2
This is line2

$ uniq file1.txt

Output:

This is line1

This is line2

44. VI: Visual text editor

The "vi" command can be used to create a new file if it doesn't exist or to open an existing file.

Example:

$ vi file1.txt

This command creates a new file "file1.txt".

The following are some of the commands and description that be used to write or delete in a file and to exit a file.

i: This Command inserts text before cursor's current location.
I: This Command inserts text at beginning of the current line.
A: This Command inserts text at end of current line.
a: This Command inserts text after cursor's current location.
o: This Command creates a new line below cursor location.
O: This Command creates a new line above cursor location.
x: This Command deletes the characters under the current cursor location.
X: This Command deletes the characters present before the cursor's current location.
d$: This Command deletes from current cursor to the end of the line.
D: This Command deletes from the cursor to the end of the current line.
dd: This Command deletes the line where the cursor is on.
:wq This Command exits vi and save changes.
:q! This Command exits vi without saving changes.

45. WC: Print byte, word, and line counts of a file

The "wc" command is used to print counts of newlines, words and bytes for each file.

Example:

$ wc file1.txt

Output:

10 23 700 file1.txt

Where 10 is the number of lines, 23 is the number of words, and 700 is the number of characters for file "file1.txt".

46. ECHO: Display message on screen

The "echo" command is used display a line of text.

Example:

$ echo UNIX Commands!

Output:

UNIX Commands!

47. EXPR: Evaluate expressions

The "expr" command is used to evaluate an expression to corresponding output value.

Example:

$ expr 5=5

Returns 1 (true) if the expressions are equivalent or 0 (false) if they are not. Here, the values 5 and 5 are equal, and therefore equivalent, so the output will be: 1

48. PRINTF: Format and print data

The "printf" command is used to print a formatted string to the standard output.

Example:

$ printf 'Hello\nWorld\n!'

Output:

Hello
World
!

49. GREP: Search file(s) for lines that match a pattern

The "grep" (global regular expression) command is used to search one file or multiple files for lines that contain a pattern.

Example:

$ grep string file1

This command will display all the lines containing the text as "string" in file1

50. HELP: Display information about built-in commands

The "help" command is used to display information about built-in commands.

Example:

$ help echo

This command will display a brief description of the built-in shell command "echo".

51. CAL: Display a calendar

The "cal" command is used to display formatted calendar from the command line.

Syntax: cal [options] [[[day] month] year]

Examples:

$cal

Displays calendar of current month.

$ cal 04 2015

Displays the calendar for April of the year 20015.

$ cal 2015

Displays the calendar of whole year. i.e. 2015.

52. CANCEL: Cancels a print job

The "cancel" command is used to exit print jobs. The -a option will remove all jobs from the specified destination.

Example:

$cancel

Cancels all pending print jobs.

53. EXIT: Exit the shell

The "exit" command is used to terminate running jobs and cause the shell to exit.

Example:

$exit

Common aliases for exit are: "bye", "logout", and "lo".

54. GZIP/GUNZIP: Compress/ Decompress files(s) to and from zip format

The "gzip" command can be used to compress the files and "gunzip" command can be used to decompress the files.

Example:

$ gzip file1

This command compresses the file1 with .gz extension.

Example:

$ gunzip –d file1.gz

This command decompresses the file1.

55. DATE: Display the date and time

The "date" command is used to display the current date including the time.

Example:

$ date

Output:

Wed Jun 3 10:12:26 EST 2015

56. TTY: Print filename of terminal on stdin

The "tty"command prints the file name of the terminal connected to standard input

Example:

$ tty

Output:

/test/pts/2

57. HEAD: Output the first part of file(s)

The "head" command is used to display the first N number of lines in a file. By default, it prints the first 10 lines of a file.

Example:

$ head file1.txt

This command will display the first 10 lines of file "file1.txt".

$ head -7 file1.txt

This command will display the first 7 lines of file "file1.txt".

58. TAIL: Output the last part of files

The "tail" command is used to display the last N number of lines in a file. By default, it prints the last 10 lines of a file.

Example:

$ tail file1.txt

This command will display the last 10 lines of file "file1.txt".

$ tail -7 file1.txt

This command will display the last 7 lines of file "file1.txt".

www.ingramcontent.com/pod-product-compliance
Lightning Source LLC
Chambersburg PA
CBHW060938050326
40689CB00013B/3142